SOCIAL WORK IN 42 OBJECTS *(and more)*

curated by **Mark Doel**

Social Work in 42 Objects *(and more)*

Curated by Mark Doel

First published by Kirwin Maclean Associates Ltd in 2017

First edition 2017 ISBN: 978-1-903575-93-2

A catalogue for this book will be available from the British Library

Kirwin Maclean Associates Limited,
4 Mesnes Green, Lichfield, Staffordshire

ISBN: 978-1-903575-93-2

Printed in Great Britain

THANKS

The *Social Work in 40 Objects* blog relied entirely on the interest and support of everyone kind enough to propose an object and share something of their own relationship with social work. Thank you.

I put out early feelers to see if *40 Objects* made sense, and I am especially grateful to Liz Allam, Avril Bellinger, Deirdre Ford, Catherine Gray and Julie Mann, who amply demonstrated its feasibility and gave much encouragement.

I received help to consider technical options for the project, especially from Tarsem Singh Cooner and Simon Cauvain, and I am indebted to Raj Allam for setting in place the mechanics of the blog. Positive comments about the blog's look belong entirely to him.

My sincere thanks to all those who publicised the blog, tweeting and the like, to reach as many interested persons as possible; to Luke Stevenson for including a piece in Community Care online; and to Reineth Prinsloo for a magnificent job encouraging no less than eight students in Pretoria, South Africa, to propose objects.

I gratefully acknowledge the forbearance of those whose Objects entered *the collections* - with just 50 words for the descriptive 'plaques'. This tested the *less is more* principle.

How fortunate I have been to find ethical publishing and the supportive involvement of Siobhan Maclean, to whom I give sincere thanks. Thanks, also, to Ashley Core and Carl Joice.

My heartfelt thanks to Jan Doel for providing the initial spark for this book.

IMAGE CREDITS

Compass of shame: Nathanson, D (1992) *Shame and Pride : Affect Sex and the Birth of the Self*, VW Norton & Co.
Computer: *Luke Jones, IBM PC (CC BY 2.0)*.
Court hat: *grateful thanks to Leah Woffenden, Sheffield Theatres*.
Foundling hospital token: *Coram*.
The Falcon: *Marvel Comics*.

All other images have been created by the Object proposer or by Mark Doel; or are freely available as far as enquiries have determined.

The objects in this book are a gift to social work from all those who have proposed them. This book is also a gift. When you buy it, be aware that profits from sales will go to NGO TARA Homes for Children in Delhi, India, to support work with street children.

SOCIAL WORK IN 42 OBJECTS *(and more)*

SOCIAL WORK IN 42 OBJECTS *(and more)*

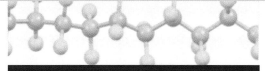

FABRIC OF SOCIAL WORK

1 Foundling hospital token
2 School bag
□ *cushion* □ *lappieskombers*
□ *ball of wool* □ *kete* □ *khurjini*
□ *hammock*

PLACE AND SPACE

□ *house* □ *foundations*
□ *cardboard box* □ *labyrinth*
□ *enigma* □ *puzzle* □ *trypillian spiral*
□ *panopticon* □ *compass*
□ *mind the gap*

3 Outline of a house
4 Patch office door
5 A-Z street finder
6 Real-life library

TOOLS OF THE TRADE

□ *blackboard* □ *chandelier*
□ *juggling balls* □ *tennis ball* □ *eyes*
□ *glasses* □ *compass (shame)*
□ *condoms* □ *hammer*
□ *box of spanners*

7 Work bag
8 Memory jar
9 Cue / Radical Social Work
10 Teflon

SOCIAL WORK AT TABLE

□ *stove* □ *cheese fondue* □ *green cup*
□ *coffee cup* □ *anchor mug* □ *tea pot*
□ *scales* □ *paper plates*
□ *paperweight* □ *pint of beer*
□ *bottle of coke* □ *ice lolly*

11 Tamada
12 Food
13 Chinese bowl
14 Round table

CLOTHING SOCIAL WORK

15 Jane Addams' coat
16 Court hat
17 Ileke ibile
18 Button
19 Grey blanket
□ *jeans* □ *sandals* □ *shoes* □ *mitten*
□ *jewellery*

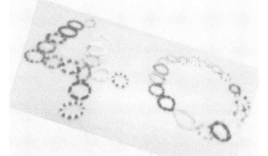

SOUNDS OF SOCIAL WORK

20 Mouthpiece
21 Drum
□ *violin* □ *guitar* □ *vinyl* □ *miserere*
□ *songs*

SOCIAL WORK ON THE MOVE

22 Traffic sign
23 Lego aeroplane
24 Car jack, lug wrench
□ bike □ bicycle □ car □ car badge
□ bus □ mobile garden

DOCUMENTING SOCIAL WORK

□ magna carta □ hogarth's coram
□ manchester box □ kennedy report
□ cartoon by kal □ whose welfare
□ mental health act
□ care guidelines □ first clare

25 Stan and Beveridge
26 School entrance sign
27 Riad's identity card

FUNDING SOCIAL WORK

28 Crown coin
29 Handful of coins
30 Budget

COMMUNICATING SOCIAL WORK

□ notebooks □ radio
□ computer □ iPod □ baby monitor
□ selfie

31 Mobile phone

GIFTS AND MEMENTOES

□ book stand □ letter opener □ cane
□ bard on a brick □ ceramic sculpture
□ esculape □ kembang

32 Postman Pat
33 Crib
34 Keys (female and male)

NATURAL WORLD

35 Bella
36 The Falcon
□ fish net □ trees □ bonsai □ cork

DYSTOPIA / UTOPIA

37 Yellow star
38 Dalek
39 Cross
40 Candle
41 Hour glass
□ band aid □ insurances
□ walking stick □ pen □ umbrella
□ heart
42 Your Object

SOCIAL WORK IN 42 OBJECTS *(and more)*

bjects are a significant part of our life, even helping to shape who we are.

We want to take care of *things.* I still treasure my teddy bear from early childhood; I don't derive my identity from this bear and could survive its loss, but there is an attachment to it as something that was 'not-me' - Winnicott's notion of a *transitional* object. Its continuity as a keep-sake during my life endows it with a personal significance that transcends mere materialism.

Whole cultures are known through their objects – artefacts that in some instances might be the only way in which we now understand anything about them, perhaps even their very existence. We have one such artefact in this collection, *Trypillian spiral,* which decorates a pot from an ancient Moldovan civilisation.

If anthropologists from a post-apocalyptic future were seeking evidence of the nature of a social work tribe, even its very existence, what might this be?

When I decided to open a blog called *Social Work in 40 Objects*, I was uncertain whether it would chime. Could an abstraction like social work be illustrated by something as concrete as objects, the professional equivalents of teddy bears?

Social work is an especially diverse and contested idea. Can it, then, find an expression through objects? Whereas the scales of justice and a judge's gavel might come readily to mind as symbols of the law, or a stethoscope and a thermometer for medicine, there is nothing so hard and fast for social work. If asked to design a road traffic sign, *Social Work Ahead,* it's a struggle to imagine how that might look.

No *single* Object, then, can be expected to stand in place for social work as a whole, a material synecdoche; but *a collection* of objects might be capable of representing a more complete, inclusive social work. Perhaps such a collection, drawn from a wide range of people, could aspire to be more illuminating than the ready icons for law and medicine?

The search for objects to reveal larger stories has become quite the trend. Neil MacGregor selected artefacts from the vast collection of the British Museum to tell a *History of the World in 100 Objects*. Indeed, museums now organise their displays into coherent and engaging narratives, sometimes via a tight selection of a few select objects, along a Bauhaus principle of *less is more.* A limited collection of objects is a popular device to help visitors avoid being fatigued by the vast choice of things.

The selection of objects can be descriptive, as in MacGregor's *100,* or an exploration of identity, like Fintan O'Toole's *History of Ireland in 100 Objects;* or, in the case of Sherry Turkle's *Evocative Objects,* 'companions to our emotional lives, provocations to thought'.

Could *40 Objects* achieve more than a mere display and evoke a social work identity, 'a provocation to thought'?

Might an appeal to a diverse group of people's creative powers conjure a social work that goes beyond dry, textual accounts and leaden definitions?

My uncertainty about *40 Objects* was answered by a carillon of objects ringing loud and clear: 127 all told. From the 1950s reality of *Bella* to the abstraction of *Real-life library,* the narratives that accompanied the objects were enriched by the stories of the people who proposed them.

Those proposing objects for the collection came from diverse backgrounds and various relationships with social work: social workers, educators, current and former service users, managers, policy makers, researchers, publishers, other professionals - and plenty who straddled many of these categories.

'Donors' of objects came from 24 countries across five continents, with some success in reaching beyond the English-speaking world.

Curating the objects

With 127 objects available to this social work exhibition, how best to display them? If this were a physical exhibition of artefacts, various rooms would house collections of objects illustrating different themes; in this spirit I set about arranging the objects into smaller collections.

I'd first thought to elicit themes from the stories that accompanied each object, but most objects supported many themes.

In a Zen way, the path ahead made itself clear: look to the objects *as Objects* and let them group themselves. In the main these clusterings did sort themselves. Different social work themes were reintroduced from one collection to another, but I hope you will agree that this is of no matter; indeed, it becomes a strength.

The final collection (*Dystopia/Utopia*) is the only one that is determined by a superimposed theme rather than by the nature of the objects as objects.

As curator, I take responsibility for the way in which the collections are gathered and displayed in their 'cabinets'. I hope you enjoy them. In selecting the numbered Objects (the 42), my aim is to achieve a balanced, diverse collection overall.

The power of objects

As I was collecting these objects, I came across a box of artefacts in a museum - spices, raw materials, carved items - all of which were used by Thomas Clarkson in the late 18th century in the campaign to abolish slavery. 'Clarkson's Box' spoke more directly to people than fine words. Perhaps a 'box' of social work objects could counter public ignorance of social work?

The objects in Clarkson's Box were powerfully immediate, but they required an accompanying text to reveal their full story. Similarly, our objects need a side plaque to help the viewer align them with a vision of social work. The ambiguity of the objects enables observers to make their own interpretations, and this is part of their charm. Learning a little about the social work journey of the people proposing the object also helps us to imagine a biography for that object.

SOCIAL WORK IN 42 OBJECTS (and more)

Bricolage

If this were a physical museum of social work and these objects were solid artefacts rather than images in a book, they could be reassembled into different collections from time to time: a form of *bricolage,* in which a closed set of objects is recombined to evoke new and different perspectives and feelings. This way, we could hope to attract first-time and returning visitors to find something new from each shake-up.

If we were to rearrange all of these things, exchanging the numbered objects with objects currently in the 'cabinets', to revamp the same set of 127 objects, what alternative themes could inspire this new arrangement? How about these five collections:

1 Metaphor

About half of the objects in the full collection manage some metaphorical allusion to social work. Many are purely so, like *Cushion* and *Radio*; a quick count suggests about forty whose primary purpose is as metaphor and, as such, call for some interpretation. For instance, the relationship between social work and *Car jack, lug wrench* needs a deciphering text; once the cipher is available the object becomes meaningful and entertaining.

Objects like *Cardboard box* are presented as *analogous*, in that the relationship to social work is compared in a way that throws new light on both. The brevity of the narrative for the cabinet objects means we viewers must do some of the heavy lifting to find our own meanings.

2 Personal

Forty or so objects arise from the direct experiences of the proposer, sometimes powerfully combining the personal and the professional, like *Mouthpiece*. The personal objects have deep symbolic meaning for the proposer and gain evocative power when we can relate that personal experience to our own.

We don't need to stand beneath that *Chandelier* to understand how an object can become a magnet for the memories of a fraught episode, and the lasting professional learning that derives from it.

Postman Pat might seem a very personal object located in a specific time and place, yet *as an object* it is a perfect contemporary example of the *Lares* – the Roman household gods. They protected their local environment as surely as *Postman Pat* has looked out for its owner, Sheila, and her workplace.

3 Practical

Some objects presented for the collection are ones that social workers deploy in their everyday work. They are not so numerous as you might expect to find in many other jobs, especially trades like plumbing or upholstery, where implements are important. There are about twenty such practical objects in this collection, such as *Drum, Condoms,* and *Notebooks.* What has been called the 'paraphernalia of everyday practice' can be lost because of its ordinariness. Time, then, to retrieve these paraphernalia?

4 Historical

About twenty objects draw explicitly on aspects of social work's history, such as *Foundling hospital token, Jane Addams' coat, Kennedy report* and *Crown coin.* Indeed, my first thoughts about gathering objects had been that these would trace social work's history. Happily, this narrow idea became much broader.

5 Socio-political

The struggle between the values of social work and the political realities is not easily represented in an object, though several in this collection symbolise and highlight the political dimension - past (*Green cup*) and present *(Grey blanket)*, the hegemony of neoliberalism *(Stan and Beveridge)* and enduring poverty *(Food)*. Others do this more implicitly, such as *Panopticon* (leading us to consider the pros and cons of surveillance), *Blackboard* (concerning the commodification of the public realm) and *Jeans* (a take on the growth of managerialism and a generational perspective on social work).

360° perspective

This project has never been value neutral. Its aim is to give expression to *who and what social work thinks it is* and, as such, to stand up for social work. I hope it will encourage more discussion about social work *outside* the ranks of the profession, encouraging people who don't know much about social work to get more aware and more involved.

Any collection should provide an all-round view. *Yellow star* is an indictment of what social work and other professionals are capable of when they become hand-maidens of an oppressive regime (or, less dramatically, cold-eyed state functionaries); positively viewed, it's a warning of the dangers of abandoning the core values of social work in the face of powerful élites.

The idealism that supports many of the objects is inspiring; however, like *Scales,* it needs to be balanced with a clear-eyed awareness of the realities of practice and policy and the rough edges of experience.

Object 42

I hope you will take up the invitation to bring your own object to the Exhibition. The empty plinth at Object 42 awaits your nomination and, of course, an expository plaque about you and the story of your object.

If you would like more information about the objects and proposers, visit the website:

socialworkin40objects.com

FABRIC OF SOCIAL WORK

Male C

Xmas Charles

11 Febry 1767

Harriet chose Foundling hospital token …

… because these tokens represent an enduring theme in social work – separation and loss, particularly those with fractured hearts towards the bottom of the token. The tokens were chosen by parents; they provided a unique opportunity to allow them to express, if only symbolically, their point of view. Some parents revealed nothing – they simply tore a strip off the clothes they were wearing, but others painstakingly embroidered initials and hearts on their tokens, or left the child with a piece of jewellery or a coin, presumably hoping that this might serve as a memento even if they were never reunited.

The tokens can be seen as emblems of the pain incurred when parents and children cannot live together, even when the separation is necessary and clearly in the interests of the child – many of the Foundling Hospital infants would have been abandoned or died of starvation had they not been admitted. None of the Foundling Hospital children saw their tokens again after they had been admitted – they were filed away, their potential significance for the children unacknowledged and lost.

Young people in care value personal possessions – Objects – that link them to home. Such objects symbolise a continuity between the past and the present, yet research finds that many carers fail to appreciate their significance and these *cherished objects* are often lost.

A scrap of material left by a mother who placed her baby in the Foundling Hospital in 1767.

The Foundling Hospital (which continues today as Coram) was founded by Thomas Coram in 1739. It is the oldest British children's charity.

Harriet Ward

I spent several months as a community service volunteer, in a children's home. It was not a very good home (it closed down soon afterwards) and many of the staff and the children were unhappy, but it was a result of that experience that I became a social worker. I travelled from practice to research, undertaking empirical studies to inform policy and practice, exploring questions such as when it might be legitimate for the state to intervene in family life.

Ludovic Barillot
I am an educateur, a member of the family of social work professions. For 14 years I lived and worked on the Ile de Réunion in the Indian Ocean where I created a volunteer association, 'Arts et Traditions'. Its aim was, and is, to develop the potential of disadvantaged people through the production of local crafts, such as curtains, bags, drumsticks, table settings. These can be started up with no financial assistance and are sustainable.

*Ludovic chose **School bag** ...*

... because my son wore this school bag daily to school in Réunion and he still has the bag to this day. It was made within the *Arts et Traditions* association.

When I arrived from France in Réunion in 1970 I sensed a culturally degraded situation, a society of Planters in an old colony, but changing and aspiring to a Western lifestyle. Whatever one's place in this society it felt devalued and not self-reliant. There was huge importation from France and an economic monoculture of sugar, with massive unemployment and lack of qualifications.

Large sections of the population desired change: to live differently, and earn an income from their own activity. It is in this context that *Arts et Traditions* was created to develop production of small domestic crafts

that required traditional know-how, and to develop this production through exhibitions and the like, which would bring income for the creators. The membership grew quickly, the status of families in difficulty strengthened markedly as they became authors of their own destiny. There was a strong and growing demand for these hand-made products and people who had been dependent developed new relationships with each other, the wider community and with traditional culture.

The social workers involved were seen as community activists but without losing their 'original' role as social and educational action professionals.

Arts et Traditions continues, 40 years on. Craft production has diversified and exhibitions are well-received. The poorest families testify that it is "life changing".

FABRIC OF SOCIAL WORK *COLLECTION*

cushion	**lappieskombers**	**ball of wool**	**kete**	**khurjini**	**hammock**

cushion	lappieskombers	ball of wool	kete	khurjini	hammock
The more a cushion is used the softer it becomes, just as trust builds over time between client and social worker. *A cushion may become worn out, its covers replaced, but it's still a cushion; people may have problems but they will always have an inherent worth.*	*Each piece of the lappieskombers (Afrikaans for quilt) is beautiful but when they are sewn together they become something yet more wondrous.* *Good social work is multi-professional and I see the pieces of the quilt as the coming together of many people to empower clients.*	*Like the web that spiders spin, a ball of wool represents the knitting of a support network in social groupwork. The group as a social support network is a very significant aspect of social work practice and it's important to know how to 'knit' these networks.*	*A kete is a woven flax bag. A basket of knowledge of aroha [Maori for love], peace and the arts and crafts which benefit the Earth and all living things.* *Kete provides constant refreshment for social workers in their quest for self-knowledge, skills and values.*	*Khurjini is a kind of Georgian saddle-bag. Like Santa's sack it's full of sweet things and warm clothes that bring pleasure and comfort. There's often something unexpected, too, brought out of a Khurjini. Its owner can be creative and spontaneous, like good social work.*	*What better way than a hammock to represent the holding environment so central to social work? We trust a hammock that is strong and well-grounded; we allow it to enfold us so we can rise a little above our situation without fear of falling, from where we can reflect.*
Kgomotso Ntlatleng	Marla Grové	Yolanda Domenech	Liz Beddoe	Nino Shatberashvili	Ann Bergart

PLACE AND SPACE

PLACE AND SPACE *COLLECTION*

house

A house is where most family social work is done. It is a realistic place, not an idealistic environment, and often the work is done in poor home settings.

It can be challenging to work in the family home: family members are not always waiting at the door welcoming their social worker!

Roberta Motiečienė

foundations

Buildings change with renovations, restructurings and new inhabitants; for me, it is social work that provides the stable foundations, the constant values, whatever happens in the wider world.

This keeps me motivated in these times of remorseless change.

Julia Wheeler

cardboard box

Like social work, a cardboard box has wonderful but often underestimated potential. it can shelter, make a game, be a useful way to move and keep things. A lost-and-found box cares for the abandoned, neglected, forgotten - and for a homeless person on a cold night, it saves a life.

Martin Camiré

labyrinth

Taking time to walk the safe, contained space of this floor Labyrinth enables people to find themselves. The courage to stay on the path, through twists and turns, even when we are unsure of its destination is a mark of true 'grit', both personally and professionally.

Bernard Moss

enigma

When and from where we walk into Escher's Enigma will determine what we see: it reminds us that not everything is as it seems and, depending on perspective, we all see things differently. The dynamics and direction of travel are highly complex and not immediately known.

Angie Lewis

puzzle

When I work with children they are like individual pieces of a puzzle who may not seem to 'fit' in; through groupwork I start to see a larger picture, how they might all fit together. By making connections we are making one whole puzzle picture - it's both a frustrating and joyful process.

Žaneta Šerkšnienė

trypillian spiral

The spiral is a symbol of conflict and dialectical process, very apt for social work. It is preserved in many artefacts of ancient Trypillian culture in Moldova.

Ancient cultures can be harnessed to social work to develop Social Wellness in deprived regions.

Eugeniu Rotari

panopticon

Bentham's Panopticon is a place from where you can see all. It speaks to self-regulation and surveillance in social work; how to help parents and communities to develop self-regulation and appropriate watchfulness, while at the same time avoiding the sinister elements?

Caroline McGregor

compass

For social workers with clients and for social policy makers the main thing is to determine the right direction towards social and personal well-being. A kind of professional compass is needed for this - and one that also provides security for society in the widest sense of this notion.

Boris Shapiro

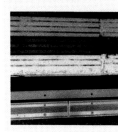

mind the gap

How to mind the gap between idealism and reality and bridge the gap between various sections of society: 'one foot in the establishment and one amongst the poor'. Gaps join as well as separate.

We social workers mind (take care of and also worry about) this gap.

Mark Doel

Outline of a house

Catherine Gray
As a publisher in the field of social work for over 20 years, I deal with outline ideas all the time. An outline is just a beginning. It is an idea that can be subjected to scrutiny and interrogation, a plan that can be adapted and revised.

*Catherine chose **Outline of a house** …*

… because social workers work with many forms of outline, diagrammatic and verbal. Some are descriptive in function, some serve the purpose of an agenda or checklist. I like the outline of a house because it encapsulates both human need and human aspiration. It appeals to our sense of the universal.

In outline form, a house symbolises what Gaston Bachelard calls 'our corner of the world' – a place we can be ourselves in and to which we can always return. It also invokes the material space of people's lives which carry the traces of our actions and relationships.

Typically, a house is one of the first things a child might learn to draw. So the outline of a house can be a tool for social workers talking to children about the significant figures and events in their lives, what makes them feel safe or scared.

Indeed, the idea of a house speaks powerfully across the life course: to young adults aspiring to have a home of their own, families on the move across continents fleeing bombs, hunger and terror, or old people fearful of giving up their houses to go into care or struggling with isolation living alone.

Of all the professions, social workers understand the secrets of houses, what acts of love, care, violence or neglect can be hidden behind their walls.

In our age of insecurity, cut-backs and crisis, we may be constrained by resources but not by empathy or imagination. For social work the outline of a house encapsulates a form of aspiration and a call for social change.

*Annie chose **Patch office door** ...*

... because it reflects a moment in the history of social work in England. No. 52 Doughty Street London WC1 was the *patch office* for the southernmost part of Camden; three teams covering three small geographical areas. Following the reforms recommended by the Seebohm report, we covered all client groups. We were 'generic social workers' - community workers one day, dealing with fostering or mental health issues the next.

We got to know our areas well and could respond to changes such as the arrival of Bangladeshi families joining their menfolk who worked in the restaurants. The families were helped by a community programme to manage the change from rural life to settling in the heart of London. Then there was the 'posh' club that tried to connect lonely, increasingly disabled academics who lived in isolating bedsits.

Our caseloads included cradle to grave and if I am honest the young families I had on my caseload got a better deal than other client groups as that was where my interest lay.

What was great was having resources in the same building, such as the council-run home help service - so a quick journey up or down the stairs could lead to finding out how someone was getting on after a hospital stay. Not many clients had phones and had to be contacted by letter.

Now social work is specialised and a family can have different social workers involved depending on the needs of people in the household. No doubt there will be calls for a more joined-up approach.

And the door at Number 52 now leads to commercial offices for literary agents. Times change.

Annie Marsh I fell into social work when I took a year off in the middle of my degree studies, then I was a social work trainee in Camden, London. I worked for 32 years in the Adoption team in Sheffield.

A-Z street finder

*Liz chose **A-Z street finder** …*

... because it was my constant companion. I covered a large geographical patch in East Birmingham (the English Midlands) and – in the days before satnavs and Google Maps – it was essential for navigating to the homes of the service users with whom I was working. I remember some frustrating 'tear my hair out' moments when I had overrun my last visit, trying to find my way to the next, pulling over in my little red Vauxhall Corsa, hazard lights flashing, whilst I pored over the map, trying to work out where I was. The roads and networks of that area gradually became familiar – and slowly I became less dependent on my trusty A-Z.

In a metaphorical sense the A-Z represents how as social workers we were expected to do a bit of everything, to cover it all, from A-Z. In my time I have made sandwiches, helped people cook meals, clean their houses and write letters; I have accompanied people to court, hospitals, police stations, cinemas, taught English, attended funerals, created and led groups. I have advocated, advised, supported, mediated, challenged, facilitated and trained.

It is something that I love about social work, that you are a jack of all trades and can offer the support that a person actually needs, whatever that may be (though I accept it is getting more difficult).

The A-Z makes me think about how each service user is located within a particular context. When you look at where they live on the map, it reminds me that each person is linked to a wider network – a family, a neighbourhood, a local community and ultimately society itself. It makes me reflect on how the circumstances in which people finds themselves are inextricably tied up with this wider context and that, as social workers, it is vital that we acknowledge it and incorporate it in our work. And the A-Z leads me to ask where do we place ourselves on the map?

Liz Allam

I qualified as a social worker in 2002. I have worked in a diverse range of settings, including mental health, with homeless people, in statutory and voluntary organisations, as well as with children in Delhi, and more recently as a Mental Health Advisor supporting unemployed people. Currently I'm on maternity leave from my social work position at Farleigh Hospice in Essex, England, working with people affected by illness and bereavement.

John Dow

We service users are looking for (longing for?) social workers who can deliver the type of personalised services that I, and others like me, need. What do social workers themselves need in order to guide and influence them? Well, they need to be able to rely on all the knowledge and information at their disposal from libraries and other sources that keep them informed so they know what service users and carers like me need. But how do I and others like me fit into this continual search for knowledge?

*John chose **Real-life library** …*

… because I believe that I am the 'real-life reference library' - as are all the other people who need to use social work services.

We need to be 'accessed' alongside all of the books, publications, policy documents and regulations. We can be this *real-life library* (who won't charge you or fine you for late returns), who will be a library of real life information. We can all begin to see proper partnership and from this, real and sustainable influence from our involvement.

We can together continue on our journey as key, valued partners - service users and social workers together - and begin to see real, personalised services where we appreciate each other's passion, knowledge and commitment to delivering the social work services that are needed and wanted.

TOOLS OF THE TRADE

TOOLS OF THE TRADE *COLLECTION*

blackboard	chandelier	juggling balls	tennis ball	eyes	glasses

blackboard

I'm a teacher in the Netherlands. There is education in social work, but too little social work in education; the blackboard symbolises this gap.

Schools have become businesses, and education has become instruction. Social workers find themselves repairing the damage.

Hilda Baar-Kooij

chandelier

Every time I see this chandelier hanging in the hall of the children's mental health agency where I am Director, I am reminded of the importance of relationship and mindfulness in social work: a testing incident could have resulted in it crashing down!

Andy Malekoff

juggling balls

It might be obvious, but the ability to keep various balls in the air at the same time is a real skill and necessary for survival in social work.

It's not just a metaphor - I keep these balls to practise my own juggling. I find them to be a great stress buster.

Jonathan Parker

tennis ball

A joint appointment between health and social services also meant membership of a multidisciplinary tennis team!

As the social worker I was the link for clients between a number of services, all of which were important to them, and coordination was made easier by team playing.

Jane Monach

eyes

As a social worker I observe harsh circumstances, I see sadness, despair, anger, conflict: I see all that in people's eyes. I convey empathy; I look for opportunities; my eyes show determination in the face of discrimination.

What I see helps me engage; what they see gives hope.

Reineth Prinsloo

glasses

Not consciously at first, but I now know that I use my glasses as a statement: they are me.

They're a talking point, which was always a good start in my social work with older people.

My glasses are a plea to express yourself and to celebrate diversity in the world.

Karen Heycox

compass (shame)

Knowing and understanding the 'Compass of Shame' has helped me identify and respond to the expression of shame both within myself and in others.

It has enhanced my relationships with people and enriched my professional career, as practitioner and social work educator.

Majella Hickey

condoms

Condoms were an essential tool of our trade in sexual health education and HIV prevention in the clinic where I worked for over 15 years. They remind me of the positive aspects of social work in the dark days of AIDS and of a very rewarding time in a multi-disciplinary team.

Maeve Foreman

hammer

An incident in which a client threatened a social worker with a hammer reminds me of the need for courage in social work and how this quality tends to be underestimated.

Social workers often have to respond to threatening situations with nothing available other than their own wits.

Nigel Parton

box of spanners

I don't like 'tools' in social work, as it implies we are fixing some part, rather than working with the person as a whole.

Instead of using tick box lists, far better to sit listening to a person's story. Social work is a human process, so let's put away that toolbox.

Malcolm Payne

*Prospera chose her **Work bag** …*

… because it reminds me about my days in social work practice.

This bag is significant because it was what I used when I worked in an English local authority social work team. Its contents have a few reminders of the work I did then - my staff ID card, a few receipts and bits of paper from that time. The bag is worn in parts, perhaps indicative of how worn out I was at the point I made the decision to become a social work educator.

The significance of retaining the bag for me indicates hope and facilitates reflection, two key components of social work.

Bags are used by many to hold valuable personal items and can also be considered as part of one's image. Work bags may also contain important work-related documents and items. I never left home without it.

So, this is my social worker bag; it's been zipped up and put away for about 11 years but still holds clear memories of the days when it was at my side as my faithful companion and contained all that I regarded as necessary to enable me carry out the daily tasks of working with children who are in our care.

Prospera Tedam

I had some understanding of justice and injustice and believed that by studying law I could contribute to making the world a better, fairer place. Unsuccessful in my law application at the University of Ghana, I was offered social work, a new course. I wasn't convinced that this was for me: how would it assist me in achieving my aims; wasn't it a 'hobby' for your spare time? But soon I became aware that I could change the world through social work and 20 years later I have no regrets and have completed my doctorate, researching the experiences of Black social work students on placement.

Suzy Croft

Social workers work with people who are often at the most vulnerable time of their lives; they also face the challenge of working with, and dealing with the effects of, those who are prepared to abuse others. Every day social workers make the most complex decisions in areas where answers are seldom black and white, whilst supporting the service user's rights. I am proud to be part of the profession that is social work.

*Suzy chose **Memory jar** ...*

... because it represents some of the most poignant but also the most positive moments of my social work in the hospice.

As part of our Children's Days for bereaved children, which we hold in the hospice, we ask the children to make a memory jar.

The coloured layers in the jar are made by rubbing chalk into salt and we ask the children to make a colour that represents a memory of the person in their life who has died. At the end of the session the children usually choose to tell each other what the colours represent and in that way they talk about the person who has died.

I vividly remember one six year old Sri Lankan girl whose mum had died. She had only been in the UK for a short time and neither of her carers could speak English so she had had to do a lot of interpreting for them.

During the Children's Day she took several others under her wing, including three siblings whose mother had also died and who clearly found it very hard to talk about what had happened.

In the *Memory jar* session this little girl took the lead and described how she had a layer of brown for the colour of her mum's skin, pink because it was her favourite colour, green because their front door was green .... etc.

Memory jars are a good way for us to help bereaved children, and they teach us about the resilience of children and how they can and do survive with all that may happen to them.

We know that children can cope with life changing events, serious illness, death and dying, *if* they are given the right support and it is important that nothing that is happening in the family is hidden from them.

One of the most significant parts of my work is supporting families and children through such events and knowing that specialist palliative care social work as a profession has such an important role in the care of those who are dying and those left behind.

Radical social work and practice
Edited by Mike Brake and Roy Bailey

... because they're objects that go together like a cup and saucer, as I'll explain.

My early career was spent as a psychiatric nursing assistant in a large, old psychiatric hospital, followed by three years as a residential social worker in a reception centre on an estate in a large city.

Tensions between care and control were played out daily and it seemed odd that the least trained, worst paid work was in these most challenging situations.

Building relationships quickly was essential and I found that activities like pool were much more effective than trying to talk face to face over a table.

Social work is a *thinking* activity, reliant on theory and research and embedded in a social and ethical context. The dominant psychotherapeutic models of the time made less sense in the poverty-ridden estates from which people came.

I was struggling with the challenges that feminism was making to Marxist thought and the notion that 'the personal is political'; Brake and Bailey's book provided theoretical under-pinning for the pool cue.

Radical social work shone and faded, but for me it still provides a challenge to bureaucratic management systems.

Pete Nelson

There was a misguided dabble with becoming a solicitor until someone asked me what I was interested in - the law or people. I spent 17 years in front-line social work: 'patch'-based generic work, then child protection. Now I'm a Principal Lecturer.

Teflon is a coating spray made up of various compounds. It has a very low coefficient of friction, is highly inert, has a high melting point and wonderful electrical properties.

*Chrissie chose **Teflon** …*

… because my father is a chemist, has been for 50 years and this explains my choice of Teflon. He was a locum pharmacist and our garage was full of Victorian-style bottles of chemicals. The fascination with these bottles was heightened when he made explosions in the garden, the highlight being fireworks night. As a consequence, all this appreciation of the volatility of chemicals must have fuelled my journey into working within substance misuse.

My Teflon coating was first established when I did my placements in a medium security male prison, where I was horrified by the extreme brutality. I was asked if I had come to look for a boyfriend!

I used groupwork with armed robbers and helped to put them in touch with their bruised inner child; we were soon picking up the pieces of their Teflon coating, which proved to be only imitation.

Teflon has a high melting point and, likewise, I have not been too ruffled by offenders with serious offences and baffling histories and have not boiled over when residents tried to jump out of windows or barricaded themselves in rooms.

Teflon has remarkable electrical properties and I hope that a certain crackling wit and creativity has kept me earthed and lively in my social work practice. However, a highly insightful student did raise a note of caution: *do you think sometimes this coating and your experiences in harsh environments means the subtleties can be missed*?

All social workers need some Teflon, but maybe it's time for mine to wear a bit thinner? But this could be problematic – 'Teflon is almost unbreakable'.

Chrissie Edmonds
Volunteering with homeless young people in London propelled me into residential social work in hostels with challenging young people. Many were young care leavers or 'runaways'. After qualification, I worked at the Cotswold Community - 68 hour weeks were the norm. I set up a criminal justice project with young offenders with drug problems, then fostering and adoption. Currently I'm a Senior Lecturer and Practice Educator.

SOCIAL WORK AT TABLE

SOCIAL WORK AT TABLE *COLLECTION*

stove	**cheese fondue**	**green cup**	**coffee cup**	**anchor mug**	**teapot**

stove	cheese fondue	green cup	coffee cup	anchor mug	teapot
I grew up with very little: no access to electricity, water, sanitation. Despite the hardships, my grandmother ensured our home was warm and she cooked us meals of pap and morogo. *Social workers need to feed their service users' souls and create a caring, warm environment.*	*Group work is central to social work and preparing and eating a cheese fondue is the quintessential group experience.* *Everyone helps to set the stage (cutting the bread, lighting the lamps, opening the wine); everyone partakes of the final result.*	*I was surprised to see this green cup and saucer in a workhouse museum as it was emblematic of my early experiences of social work in a local authority. Everyone drank out of these green cups at meetings: utilitarian and egalitarian, before the coming of the barista.*	*In various coffee shops and diners, regular customers take their customary places, sometimes just nodding at one another, other times forming conversations ...* *... these moments of familiarity offer the possibility of belonging, just like good social group work.*	*My Boys Brigade mug has graced my desk for 35 years.* *Advocating for those perceived as undeserving, it's motto, 'Sure and Steadfast' has been my anchor when it's been difficult to hold firm. 'If they're giving you a hard time, you must be doing something right!'*	*I see a teapot as a metaphor for social work: a strong secure exterior to create a safe environment for the brewing; diverse flavours and capacities. Social work provides people with the necessary resources to reach their full capacity - the perfect cup of tea!*
Poppy Mashego	*Dominique Moyse-Steinberg*	*Steven M. Shardlow*	*Lorrie Greenhouse Gardella*	*Paul Johnson*	*Melinda van der Merwe*

scales	paper plates	paperweight	pint of beer	bottle of coke	ice lolly

scales

I am a 'Grow Your Own' social worker.

I chose balance scales as they best represent the need to be proportionate in our work as social workers, as well as balancing a hefty caseload and finding a balance in the reports that I write in respect of my service users.

Jillian Anderson

paper plates

We used 'social space orientation' to bring a group of adults and young people to a mutual understanding of the same social space they shared.

The youngsters were fine to be photoed but wanted to respect their privacy with Smiley 'paper plates'.

Klaus-Martin Ellerbrock

paperweight

This glass paperweight symbolises the strength, solidity and transparency of social work.

The swirls of different threads represent social work's complexity and diversity, and the way that theory and practice intertwine. And It can roll with the changes, too.

Jo Lucas

pint of beer

In years past I've supported many a service user over a pint. It symbolises normalisation and a down-to-earthness.

Strict rules have made this kind of informality somewhat frowned on, which is a shame as I think we have lost something. Or is that a half-empty approach?

Paul Stapleton

bottle of coke

Raising a son with Aspergers was a motivation to come into social work. I'm newly qualified and loving it.

A bottle of Coke is my metaphor for social work: calm and still until activated, but then capable of great fizz: rather too much of it when under pressure!

Emma Govan

ice lolly

How do you appear disarming to clients whose previous social worker got a commendation for placing a thumb between hammer and cartridge of a shot-gun?

Arriving sucking an ice lolly seemed to do the trick. This time I only had to disarm a knife.

Richard Bartholomew

|  |  |  |  |  |  |

Tamada is a person who leads the 'Supra' - a formalised festive meal, a kind of banquet. 'Supra' is an essential part of Georgian tradition, and is always accompanied by the ritual of making toasts by a toastmaster, who is Tamada.

Iago chose **Tamada** ...

... because the role of Tamada reminds me of the social worker.

Tamada is a moderator, makes initiatives ('toasts'), prevents tension and conflicts, addresses issues from one participant to another.

Tamada intervenes where a conflict emerges among participants.

Tamada provides a model, develops a kind of a pattern which is respected enough to be followed.

Tamada should be a qualified, skilful person, a charismatic personality, communicative, convincing, both logical and creative, and accomplish a therapeutic function to those who are alienated and feel like strangers.

Tamada has to be a polymath, with wide-ranging knowledge (history, poetry, literature, etc.), just like the social worker who should be a bit of everything – psychologist, lawyer, physician, sociologist, secular priest.

Tamada must be dutiful and follow the event right through to its end - there is no leaving early.

One big difference is that Tamada is almost always male, whilst social work is a more predominantly female profession. And Tamada is performing a role, whereas social workers should not become an 'outsider' to what they do. Simply said, a bad person can be a good Tamada, though never a good social worker.

Iago Kachkachishvili
I am a sociologist who calls himself an honorary social worker by virtue of being head of the Department where we first established social work education in Georgia. It became clear that these two disciplines, sociology and social work, can go together very well and hence for 10 years I am facing the charm of this collaboration.

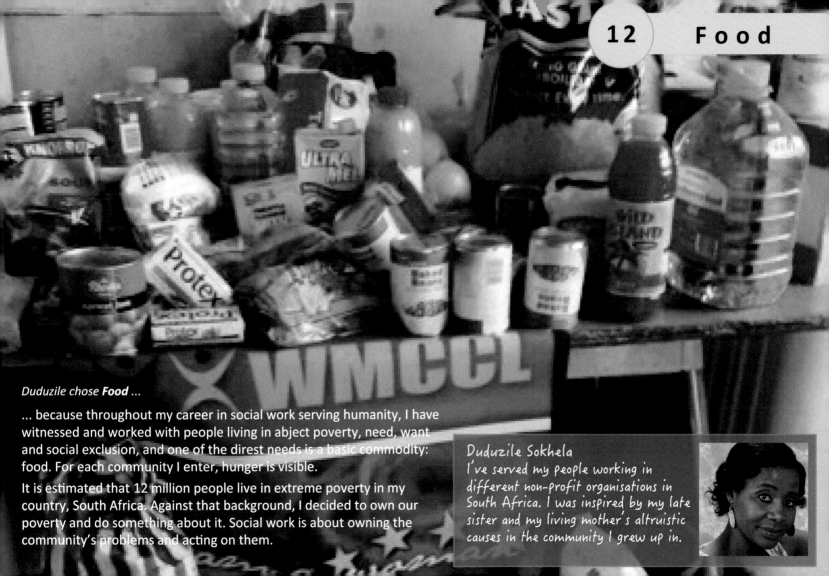

*Duduzile chose **Food** ...*

... because throughout my career in social work serving humanity, I have witnessed and worked with people living in abject poverty, need, want and social exclusion, and one of the direst needs is a basic commodity: food. For each community I enter, hunger is visible.

It is estimated that 12 million people live in extreme poverty in my country, South Africa. Against that background, I decided to own our poverty and do something about it. Social work is about owning the community's problems and acting on them.

Duduzile Sokhela
I've served my people working in different non-profit organisations in South Africa. I was inspired by my late sister and my living mother's altruistic causes in the community I grew up in.

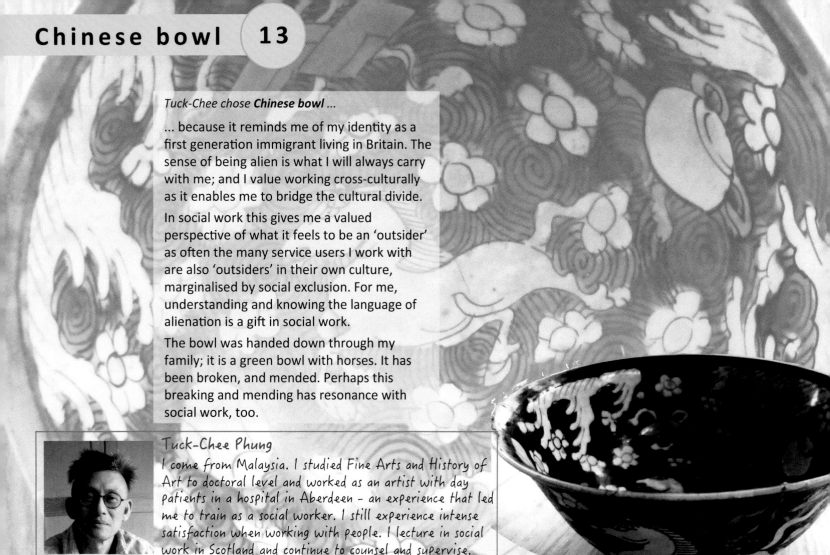

*Tuck-Chee chose **Chinese bowl** ...*

... because it reminds me of my identity as a first generation immigrant living in Britain. The sense of being alien is what I will always carry with me; and I value working cross-culturally as it enables me to bridge the cultural divide.

In social work this gives me a valued perspective of what it feels to be an 'outsider' as often the many service users I work with are also 'outsiders' in their own culture, marginalised by social exclusion. For me, understanding and knowing the language of alienation is a gift in social work.

The bowl was handed down through my family; it is a green bowl with horses. It has been broken, and mended. Perhaps this breaking and mending has resonance with social work, too.

Tuck-Chee Phung

I come from Malaysia. I studied Fine Arts and History of Art to doctoral level and worked as an artist with day patients in a hospital in Aberdeen - an experience that led me to train as a social worker. I still experience intense satisfaction when working with people. I lecture in social work in Scotland and continue to counsel and supervise.

Fabio Folgheraiter

I teach social work in an Italian University in Milan and I'm co-founder of an Italian publishing house, Edizioni Erickson Trento. I am involved in planning education and training activities in academic and fieldwork settings for social workers and social services managers. My experience is in community social work, mainly in mutual/self-help groups for people with alcohol addiction.

*Fabio chose **Round table** ...*

... because ancient Greeks and the mythical King Arthur and his knights knew very well that sitting in a circle is the best ritual for a meeting. In my view, helping people to come together freely so that they can build solutions to their life problems through dialogue is the essential core of all the social professions.

Planning meetings is one of the most important social work activities. Sitting in a circle is important here, too. At a round table no-one sits at the head. Everyone can make eye contact with each other at the same time. People are all at the same level, including the social worker.

Meeting at a round-shaped table means respecting mutuality, parity, and equality of voice. Every time a social worker tries to help people agree on shared aims, all should feel free to talk at the same level, though from a variety of perspectives.

No social work intervention should be a manipulation by an expert. This is true for multi-professional team meetings and meetings where social workers leave their offices to work with people in local communities.

The circle shape conveys parity which, in turn, evokes empowerment – the idea that people should have power to take decisions for their own lives and in their own best interests. This power is never an absolute one, but it is a good enough one.

When social workers gather people together, they should avoid having them sit at the usual angular, sharp-edged table.

Social workers should always think according to the democratic round table.

CLOTHING SOCIAL WORK

"Tolstoy, standing by clad in his peasant garb, listened gravely – but, glancing distrustfully at the sleeves of my traveling gown which unfortunately at that season were monstrous in size, he took hold of an edge and pulling out one sleeve to an interminable breadth, said quite simply that 'there was enough stuff on one arm to make a frock for a little girl', and asked me directly if I did not find 'such a dress' a 'barrier to the people'."

Jane Addams, 20 Years at Hull-House.

*Vadim chose **Jane Addams' coat** ...*

... because Jane Addams' resplendent coat is a symbol of wealth and privilege. It stands in stark contrast with the poor person's garb. The social worker who ministers to the poor from the position of power, material well-being, and authority does not empower, but relegates the needy to a secondary role in the relationship – that of an alms-taker, a charity case.

Jane Addams' coat also symbolizes the hypocrisy potential for the social worker who proclaims to uphold the values of social justice and yet lacks the self-awareness to recognize how her behavior subverts her message. This encounter with Tolstoy *(see right panel)* triggered a profound crisis in Jane Addams, a reorientation towards a more authentic and socially responsible social work practice.

Vadim Moldova

I wandered into social work after emigrating from the Soviet Union to the US, studying at Columbia University Business School, and driving a cab in New York for four years. Never looked back. Main focus now is professionalization and legitimization of social work in Moldova and post-socialist countries.

*There's a song by The Kinks (a British pop band)
– 'She's Bought a Hat like Princess Marina'*

Ruby chose **Court hat** …

… because when attending Court, female Child Care Officers (CCOs) had to be 'hatted' or they would not be permitted to the Court. None of the CCOs owned a hat, but in the Children Officers' room was a hat which we all used when attending Court. It was known as the Court hat and had not to be removed from the room except for Court duties. The hat was known as the 'Princess Marina Hat' – black, about three inches deep and comfortably sat on the top of one's head!

The Children Department at that time consisted of a Children Officer (CO), a Deputy Children Officer (DCO) and four Child Care Officers (I was one), one of whom worked part-time. All the CCOs were women, the DCO was a man.

We had to work on alternative Saturday mornings, no such thing as being paid overtime, the expectation was you finished work when you were able, but not before 5.00 pm. Tuesdays and Thursdays used to be long days: when we visited foster parents we had to see the foster father of the children fostered and at that time the local shipyards and engineering worked overtime until 8.00 pm. Foster parent visits could easily last until 10.00 at night – but you had to be in the Office by 8.30 the following day – no concessions, just expectations!

Our caseloads were quite heavy – I had 70+ cases. Home Office Inspectors used to ring the CO at approximately 4.00 pm to say they were carrying out an Inspection the following morning, when they would 'pull in' a selection of cases which they chose to examine.

One CCO absolutely hated the mandatory Court hat, but the other three of us just accepted the fact – no discussion.

Lady Almoners were early medical social workers, working in hospitals. Alongside medical assessments of patients, almoners performed what we would describe now as a 'means test' to see whether the patient needed the hospital's charity; in the process, they began to take social histories and to see patients in their wider context.

Ruby Marshall
I started my career in social work in the 1960s, initially as an almoner. Later, in 1969, I qualified as a Child Care Officer at Newcastle University, UK. I was employed as a Child Care Officer which included duties attending the local courts when I had been acting as a Guardian-ad-Litem in adoption cases.

'Ileke ibile' is the Yoruba word for Traditional bead

*David chose **Ileke ibile** …*

… because it shows the majesty of the Head of a village in Nigeria.

Social services is not a new phenomenon in Nigeria – the traditional rulers provide social welfare services through the elders and family heads among others. The traditional rulers are responsible for the maintenance of discipline and the settlement of disputes in the community and offer rewards where appropriate. Even more, they provide food for the poor, help the homeless and adopt children without families, as well as making sure there is peace and harmony in the community. The communities are highly structured to handle cases of deviance.

The traditional leaders meet the social needs of the villagers and also deal with problematic behaviors in the village and find solutions.

Today, I see social workers as wearing the *Ileke ibile,* one which cannot be physically seen or observed.

To me, the social work profession *is* the Traditional bead.

Enakele Seun David
I grew up in a small village in Nigeria where Ileke ibile is a symbol of power and caring for others. It indicates a traditional ruler in the village. As a young boy, I loved Ileke ibile and always wished to wear it because of the passion the Village Head has towards the villagers. Now I'm a social work graduate in Lithuania.

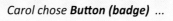

*Carol chose **Button (badge)** ...*

... because it is an iconic artifact of an exciting and ambitious project, when diverse Brooklyn constituencies living in close proximity – Polish, Irish, Latino, Black, Italian and Orthodox Jewish – faced planned shrinkage and 'red lining' (abandonment by services), in the days long before hipsters and gentrification. Rather than fighting each other over shrinking community resources, organizers trained in the model of Saul Alinsky and the Industrial Areas Foundation helped us all come together to push for a common agenda.

My community-based program provided integrated services at all levels (micro, mezzo and macro) for family wellbeing and social justice, so we were avid supporters of the COCO organizing effort. Among the great legacies came through living the 'case to cause' imperative of the social work profession – individual, group and community, personal and strategic. Most importantly, we had the opportunity to contribute to efforts that honored and addressed residents' self-expressed needs and aspirations in an effective and collaborative initiative for change.

Carol S. Cohen

Soon after returning to New York in 1974, I joined the Williamsburg-Greenpoint Human Service Center in Brooklyn, U.S. as group work supervisor and then program manager, bringing me into the Coalition of Community Organizations that made my Object - the COCO delegate button. I have never forgotten the experience, through 17 more years at Catholic Charities' programs, and my present academic career at Adelphi University School of Social Work.

*Anne chose **Grey blanket** ...*

... because blankets feature in humanitarian work with all ages as a source of warmth and comfort. Babies are swaddled in them, children tucked in beside adults in them, adults swathed in them when they have nothing else. 'But what has this to do with social work?' some might ask.

Not by choice, social workers have evolved into bureau professionals, managing individual problems rather than working on the front line of the response to urgent humanitarian crises. And yet I know I was not unusual in coming to social work with a passionate personal and political commitment to change the world.

For the first 20 years of my career, social work combined work with individuals alongside community development activities. Now, the idea of social work as being at the forefront of the current refugee crisis, for example, is not obvious.

This line of people, rescued from the sea off Lesvos, is queuing for warm, dry clothes and food before registering as refugees. Around their bare feet lie the detritus of instant comfort - empty cups of chai, wrappers from a batch of donated chocolate croissants. They hope to travel north. They are barefoot and, under the grey blankets, they are wet from wading through the sea. Their faces are not shown: they are just a few of the Nameless, desperately trying to build a new life.

Anne Hollows   After student volunteering, my 45 year social work career included work with offenders, children and families, anti-poverty campaigns and academic work. Retirement focuses on volunteer work with refugees at home and abroad, recently in Lesvos where the picture was taken. A full circle.

There are many possible explanations for these changes: professionalisation; defensiveness; individual psycho-pathologising of child protection. It is harder to identify, let alone reverse, the complex mechanisms that have allowed this to happen. The concept of 'reclaiming social work' has turned out to be both individual-specific and limited; certainly not a return to real engagement with local, national and geo-political challenges.

A key motivation of student social workers is to make a difference at the point of need. The idealism and beliefs remain with us. Social workers, current and retired, are a significant group in the volunteer force that contribute to work with refugees, though all agree that this is not 'social work' as it is presently constructed in many, perhaps most, countries.

I wonder, will we return to a time when the personal and the professional are, indeed, political?

CLOTHING SOCIAL WORK *COLLECTION*

 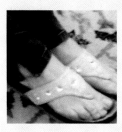   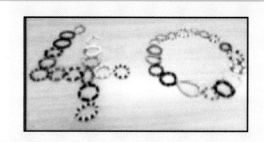

jeans	sandals	shoes	mitten	jewellery

A pair of jeans represents the time before managerialism transformed social work into a corporatised, homogenised, de-personalised, over-regulated profession. Time for the men and women in suits to give social work back to the men and women in jeans!

As a publisher, I commissioned social work books. The sandals represent the miles I know that social workers go for their clients; and they are a reminder that social workers are not exempt from a catalogue of stereo-types, including sandals and long flowing dresses!

One of my first cases taught me the importance of material help - the joy that a new pair of shoes brought to a deaf girl in a poor family.
Empathy is putting ourselves in the shoes of others.
I could walk to all of my clients, so my own shoes were always well worn.

Mitten, by Tracey Emin, was a real baby's mitten, lost and abandoned, but found by the artist, cast in bronze and now 'waving' from railings outside The Foundling Museum.
It reminds me that good social work practice can bring strength and hope to people who are lost and vulnerable.

Marilyn Bennett helped The Jewellery Group for people with learning disabilities to express social work in an Object:

Jewellery (and making it together) gave them all a sense of community, friendship and new skills.

"I love being able to make things that are personal and I can share as gifts."
"I love taking part in things, enjoy the group."
"We feel proud, really enjoy it."
"I love making bangles, seeing what they're like once they're finished, and spending time with all my friends."

Mary Thomson

Jo Burges

David Howe

Sue Taplin

Josephine, Mary, Ruth, Margaret, Nicola

SOUNDS OF SOCIAL WORK

*Simon chose **Mouthpiece** of a french horn ...*

... because the horn was one of many instruments my birth father played; his favourite. We were estranged after he and my mum divorced when I was young. I learned only recently that during this process we had a social worker who communicated with all involved ... I don't remember any of this.

I wondered about my birth father and whether he ever thought of me. I never longed for him, but felt curious – it was a gap, but not one that troubled me. Mum was open about him, shared photos, told me his strengths as well as the rest. He was a proud army band member and wrote musical scores for the range of instruments. He and his sister were adopted, but he was badly abused by his adopters. He was violent towards my mum and had problems with alcohol and drugs. She left him in order to protect my brother and me.

I decided to find him. It happened quickly; we communicated by letter and eventually met at his home. I learned of two sisters I didn't know existed. We arranged to meet again and exchanged texts.

Thirteen weeks after this he died unexpectedly. The house was burgled the evening his body was removed. My brother and I cleared his cluttered rooms and prepared for the funeral. I got to know him more through his belongings, his Objects, ones he'd never have wanted me to see. He'd had a rough time, struggling with alcohol and poverty and he'd been in prison.

He'd sold his beloved horn for cash, but the mouthpiece was something he kept and that I retrieved. It represents our respective journeys that at one seemingly insignificant point involved a social worker. It's a lasting personal reminder that 'service user' is *not* a negative term. Service users are fellow human beings who need to be *heard* not just listened to.

The mouthpiece is a metaphorical voice; the opportunity to play one's own tune rather than dance to that of another; it represents that something special that good social workers manage to find. Despite the clutter.

Simon Cauvain

I left school early, flunked sports college, worked in a gym, on building sites and in an iron castings factory. My mum was a social worker in Lincoln and, whilst it fascinated me, the last thing I wanted to do was whatever my mum did! Tired of cracking 7am ice on my water barrel as a brickie's labourer, I joined a home care company, volunteered as a befriender which led to a community care job. Now I'm a Principal Lecturer.

*Biant chose **Drum** …*

… because it has followed me every step of my way. Drawing on cultural and artistic influences from the Indian classical traditions of Guru Shishya Parampara, the drum allows me to retain a creative practice in the harsh realities of austerity, increasing bureaucracy and proceduralisation.

I have drummed my way into the heart of social work practice with individuals and community groups, communicating in the free- flowing authentic way, handling this ball of energy that is coming off the drum. The process is a leap of faith from a world of thought and reason into the world of expression. Over three decades I've intermingled social justice, music, performance and the wellbeing of people. My work takes me into many situations in many roles, not just social worker, united by a common purpose to create an inclusive environment that brings people together to feel better.

In many Shamanic societies, if you came to a medicine person complaining of being disheartened, dispirited or depressed, they would ask one of these questions:

1 When did you stop dancing?
2 When did you stop singing?
3 When did you stop being enchanted by stories?
4 When did you stop finding comfort in the sweet territory of silence?

Biant Singh Suwali

I'm a social worker and percussionist, at my happiest when combining the two. I was born and bred in the inner city of Nottingham, where my family were directly exposed to complex issues of race, poverty and disability. I grew up steeped in the traditions of Indian classical music. I chose to train as a social worker because I wanted to support people to develop their independence and make their own choices and decisions. I've worked in hospital social work departments, community mental health teams and supported young people through transition to adulthood.

SOUNDS OF SOCIAL WORK *COLLECTION*

violin	guitar	vinyl	miserere	songs
Powerful whether solo or as part of an ensemble, the violin transcends country and culture, just like social work. Playing the violin and practising social work can seem effortless, but violinists and social workers know the practise and skill that is needed for success.	No two G chords on a guitar have to have the same tone or voice. The same is true of social work. Depending on the context, our approach, training and resources, we help clients find their own voice and create wonderful new melodies out of life narratives. It takes practice.	Music brings people together. The producers of this record (Light of Love - The Miracles Club) acknowledge and build on their influences, part of a larger dialogue grounded in queer club culture. I want to bring culture and context to my social work - and boogie a little, too.	Listening to Allegri's Miserere helped with the cognitive dissonance that comes with self-knowledge that in turn arises from professional training in social work. The music eases 'head-chatter' and creates space for reflection; and that is essential for resilience.	Ala.ni's 'Cherry Blossom' reflects the optimism of the social work profession, a young child at heart. 'Darkness at Noon' is a song that speaks to the ambiguity and struggle of life and relationships, of powerful realities that social workers encounter daily.
Natia Partskhaladze	*Dana Leeman*	*Brian Kelly*	*Dave White*	*Monica Ioana Gugura*

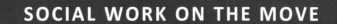

SOCIAL WORK ON THE MOVE

Sue chose **Traffic sign** ...

... because it speaks to me of the power to portray particular perspectives of 'reality' as how things are and should be – in this case, that old age is necessarily about decline, rather than growth.

It reminds me that, where dominant perspectives become ingrained, the stereotypes they support become accepted as the norm. And where this happens, a challenge to negative stereotyping is unlikely to happen without first having consciousness-raising.

But it also reminds me that we social work professionals should feel empowered to be part of the process of critically exploring taken-for-granted negative assumptions about particular groups of people. We have the skills and we have the commitment to promote social justice.

Yes, we can 'help individuals across the road' when they are experiencing difficulties - but we can do much more.

Sue Thompson
I became a social worker for a particular reason - to play my part in challenging the ageist attitudes and practices that I'd long observed as widespread in eldercare. I hope I achieve this in my work, by helping those whose right to self-determination is not being respected to fight their own battles. It's harder at a broader level, but I do my bit through my research and encouraging critical reflection via my writings.

A group of students on the MSW at NUI Galway, Ireland, built an aeroplane (Lego Serious Play) to represent social work. The new social worker (in the driving seat) and supervisor are flying to the agency. There are a number of hats on show to represent various roles, including a Top Hat for presentation at important meetings, and a crash helmet for survival in sticky situations. Jet packs on hand for a boost in confidence. The uneven steps represent the mismatch sometimes between service users needs and recent graduates knowledge.

Marguerita McGovern: Sinead, Aine, Siobhan, Rachel

*Mokgaetjie chose **Car jack, lug wrench** ...*

... because a car jack lifts vehicles for maintenance: social work is a profession that helps to lift clients from their current situation to make a positive change in their lives so that they can function better.

Maintenance is a process, whether vehicle or client. After the car jack has fulfilled its purpose the vehicle can function properly on its own. After receiving help from the social worker, clients too can live their lives independently.

Just as a lug wrench loosens and tighten nuts on car wheels, social work helps 'loosen' clients so they can express their thoughts, struggles and feelings. The helping process is not about the provision of quick solutions to problems, but building a rapport to develop trust and enter into the client's own experiential world. We help 'tighten' clients, to be strong enough to face their problems and work on them.

Mokgaetjie Mangana

I'm a social work student in Pretoria, South Africa, originally from Soshanguve township. I chose social work because it's a profession that changes lives and helps people to stand on their own feet after the social worker leaves. It's a collaborative profession that changes mindsets and empowers people; we aren't all-knowing 'experts' – we start where the client is. In the end, you just have to have a love for people and a belief that they can change their own lives. I have absolutely no doubt that social work is for me.

SOCIAL WORK ON THE MOVE *COLLECTION*

bike	bicycle	car	car badge	bus	mobile garden

bike

Working with troubled youngsters I found bike rides opened up travel to new, safer and happier locations in their troubled lives - literally and metaphorically.

The bike is simple, elegant, relies on its many parts to work properly: just like social work.

Tarsem Singh Cooner

bicycle

Too often social workers are remote outsiders, living in another world to that of those they make crucial decisions about.

The bicycle breaks down some of those barriers. What's more, you get to know the area better, the fabric of the community you serve.

Bill Badham

car

This is the same car that I've had since my student social work days. This is my 'world'. I have reflected, laughed, cried and done a lot of my job in the car, such as direct work with service users. My car acts as an office, a safe place, my space. It's vital to doing my job properly.

Caroline Pickard

car badge

I worked in a social work agency in the US in the 1970s. It was one of the most challenging times of my life and it's where I learned to question my role as a social worker. The car badge from my Rambler Estate, now a key holder, keeps me in mind of those times and the lessons learnt.

Clare Orger

bus

Life experienced on the school bus was very formative for me. Buses also touch the lives of many of my clients.

As a metaphor, I 'catch' people's own buses, I help them with the heavy loads that they carry and help them decide their destination - as driver or conductor.

Gabe Bolling

mobile garden

It's good to move away from 'fire-fighting' social work to something more creative, like mobile gardens.

Here kids and their families learn to grow things together. Through this process we engage with whole communities, not just individual families.

Eglė Celiešienė

DOCUMENTING SOCIAL WORK

DOCUMENTING SOCIAL WORK *COLLECTION*

magna carta	hogarth's coram	manchester box	kennedy report
The legal rules that underpin social work continue to evolve, sometimes in tune with social work values, other times not. *Magna Carta's* influence reinforces the importance of human rights, and reminds us all that history matters and speaks to people's lived experience.	Hogarth's works, like Gin Lane and A Rake's Progress, still form part of our social and moral consciousness. Thomas Coram, the subject of this Hogarth painting, was an early philanthropist pre-dating modern social work. His work endures in the Coram Foundation.	Clearing out my father's house, I came across this box he'd kept of all my hand-written assignments and exams from my social policy degree in '60s Manchester. It reminds me how critical social policy has been to my later social work practice and teaching.	Eileen Kennedy's report was my first exposure to the policy issues of children in Irish state care. It played a key role in the de-institutionalisation of children into foster care. I'm proud to have been a part of that process - both as social worker and foster carer.
Michael Preston-Shoot	Jane McLaughlin	Imogen Taylor	Robbie Gilligan

SOCIAL WORKER WHO TAKES CHILD FROM FAMILY

SOCIAL WORKER WHO LEAVES ABUSED CHILD WITH FAMILY

cartoon by kal

Kal (Kevin Kallaugher) illustrates how humour can communicate complex ideas and helps social workers get through the day: the 'damned if you do, damned if you don't' theme that is as relevant today as it was in 1987.

It's poignant that recurring child deaths and the ensuing crises of social work identity and confidence, do not go away.

I keep the cartoon on my notice board to remind me that the passions of the lynch mob are no way to solve complex issues.

I hope the mob stops short and says 'we were only joking - we understand you can't always get it right and you do a difficult job'.

Stephen Jordan

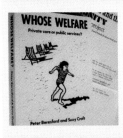

whose welfare

Whose Welfare: Private care or public services? (1986) is written from a service user perspective. It highlights the need for truly participatory policy and practice.

As a user of social work because of my mental distress, it coincided with a time I got some really good help.

Peter Beresford

mental health act

The Act, the Jones Manual, the Code of Practice and the pink forms are the tools of my mental health social work - to ensure a person's rights and dignity are protected and they and others are kept safe.

These everyday objects allow me to do a difficult job as well as I can.

Tony Deane

guidance

The NHS Continuing Care Framework (England) represents partnership working at its highest level in an area fraught with mistrust because of the high costs involved.

Partnership between health and social work services is essential if people are to receive the best services.

Anne Russell

HARRY VENNING

Harry Venning

In 1995 'Care Weekly' asked me for a cartoon; I came up with 'Clare in the Community'. I did four jokes and worried I didn't have any more cartoons in me. 'Care Weekly' folded two weeks after, so I sent the four jokes to 'The Guardian' and have been drawing Clare ever since. The 1000+ cartoons are variations on the first!

The Beveridge Report (1942) argued for social services to be universal. The UK Treasury's rejection of this idea on financial grounds continues.

*Lena chose **Stan and Beveridge** ...*

... because the lyrics to Eminem's *Stan* eloquently highlight the need for universal social services available to all at the point of need without stigma and without charge.

Had such a framework been available, a suicide causing three deaths would have been avoided and Stan, his girlfriend and baby would still be alive.

'Stan' inspired me to use its lyrics in a lecture on modern social work. Its potent message demonstrated that art can be used to substantiate social work theory and enrich its practice. The classroom's gasp over the senseless loss of life when listening to the song gave way to animated discussion about what narratives might have had a less awful ending. The students' suggestions were, they said, examples of an *unstigmatizing social work.*

Everyone with an interest in social work should revisit Beveridge, and lobby for social care to be a freely available universal service. Social work need not provide residual services focused primarily on child protection and safeguarding adults, as current neoliberal policymakers would have us believe.

Lena Dominelli
I came to social work as a community worker and trade union activist. My life experiences as a gendered, racialized woman broadened my knowledge of the world and its complexities, so that I now approach reality as socially constructed and holistic.

drawing by Lena Dominelli and Dave Whiteley

*Vesna chose **School entrance sign** ...*

... because it reflects all those fights for social work's academic status against the prejudice of other disciplines, and the long journey from 1955, when a Higher school of social work was founded in Ljubljana and provided a two-year study programme as an applied science – and finally becoming a Faculty of social work and an independent scientific discipline.

In 2015 we celebrated the 60th anniversary of social work education in Slovenia. At the end of the official programme one of the social work practitioners named Vili

Lamovšek came to the stage and gave me a present. When unwrapping it in front of the guests and friends it suddenly appeared in front of us – such a well-known sign that a lot of us remembered so well.

It had been there on the wall at the main entrance of the school of social workers from 1955 till the late 1980s when we moved to another building. Vili took it from the wall and kept it safe all those 25 years and he gave it to us to remember the past and celebrate it again as an important part of social work's history in Slovenia.

Thank you Vili.

SOCIALISTIČNA REPUBLIKA SLOVENIJA
VIŠJA ŠOLA ZA SOCIALNE DELAVCE
PRITLIČJE - LEVO

Vesna Leskošek
My mutli-professional profile (social worker, pedagogue, sociologist) is a consequence of social work's former outsider position in the Slovene scientific community, as in many others. It was 'only' recognised as an applied profession, not as an academic discipline, so students had to choose another discipline in order to achieve a degree.

Social work had no place in the socialist utopia as there was no need for social protection when class differences had supposedly been 'abolished'. However, in Yugoslavia this was recognised as an ideal not yet attained, and some form of welfare state was needed to address current social problems. Slovenia and the other states of the former Yugoslavia are unique in eastern Europe in having social work schools with such a long history - over sixty years in this case.

The sign for the entrance to the school is a symbol of social work's survival wherever it is threatened with uprooting.

*Guy chose **Riad's identity card** ...*

... because a conference of the Palestine-UK Social Work Network was hosted in Jerusalem and Riad Arar, the President of the Hebron branch of the Palestinian Union of Social Workers and Psychologists, and one of the main organisers of the conference, was not present. Riad has not been allowed by the Israeli government to enter Jerusalem, 19 miles from Hebron, since 1998.

There are about 500 Israeli army checkpoints in the West Bank and Jerusalem, and Riad can be stopped and asked to show his ID card at any one of them. One of the most difficult aspects is the apparent arbitrariness of the soldiers' decisions on restricting his freedom of movement. I have been through a checkpoint with him to visit a primary school when he was allowed through, but when taking other international delegations to visit this school (situated in the heart of an illegal Israeli settlement), Riad has been refused entry.

Principles of social justice, human rights and collective responsibility are central to social work, according to its international definition.

Who should take responsibility for the denial of the human right of freedom of movement for Riad Arar and other social work colleagues throughout the world in this kind of situation?

Guy Shennan
I'd not heard of social work until I played football with a charismatic socialist social work student and, 35 years later, the excitement of my first impressions remains. Sufficiently, in fact, to have become Chair of the British Association of Social Workers, though I've retired from football ...

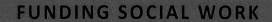

FUNDING SOCIAL WORK

*Mike chose **Crown coin** …*

… because that is the exact sum that a Hertfordshire printer, Frederick Rainer, donated in 1876 towards a fund for practical rescue work in London's Police Courts.

Offenders would be released on condition that they kept in touch with and accepted guidance from what were originally called Police Court Missionaries. In the US, John Augustus, a Boston boot maker had taken a similar initiative in the 1840s.

The development and success of this approach led to the 1907 Probation of Offenders Act that formally established the English Probation Service with a duty to 'advise, assist and befriend'

the offenders referred to them. The 1930s to 1960s saw an increasing trend towards professional casework, and after the introduction of the Certificate of Qualification in Social Work (CQSW), this became the entry requirement for new Probation Officers.

The 1990s, however, saw a dramatic shift away from a social work-based approach in England, a shift exemplified by the Conservative Prime Minister, John Major: 'Society needs to condemn a little more and understand a little less', and the Labour Prime Minister, Tony Blair: 'Tough on crime and tough on the causes of crime'. Subsequently, a social work qualification ceased to be the entry requirement for Probation work.

I'll leave you to reflect on the impact of these developments, but I am proud of the achievements of social work-trained Probation Officers in mitigating the social, emotional and financial costs of crime and imprisonment.

A crown was a British coin worth five shillings (25p)

Mike Shapton

I worked as a Probation Officer in the South Yorkshire Probation Service for 18 years until, unhappy about the changes to Probation values, I left and spent twenty years in social work education, latterly preparing social workers to work with students. I often find that social workers are unaware of the social work origins of Probation.

Putting 'Handful of coins' together has been poignant: while thinking about it, one of my old colleagues in Derbyshire died and I flew down from Scotland for the funeral. A few of our old team were at the funeral and I was telling them about my plans to contribute to 'Social Work 40 Objects'. We ended up getting the photograph done that day - the money in Jackie's hands (as it was in the taxi), another of the team taking the photograph and the money coming from the team members. So it's ended up being a real team affair.

Jane McLenachan
My first social work experiences were 'generic' - the best possible grounding for my later work as a specialist in children and family work. I soon developed an interest in practice learning and became a practice teacher before moving into social work education. I came back to Scotland in 2014.

Jane chose **Handful of coins** ...

... because it symbolises the importance of good team working and support.

Throughout my social work career, I've been fortunate to work with excellent, dedicated and supportive colleagues. This has often been an essential mechanism for coping with the stresses and pressures of the job - organisational challenges, lack of resources and the emotional impact of working with vulnerable, traumatised, abused and abusive people.

As a child protection social worker, I was undertaking parenting assessments and working with children who had been abused or considered at serious risk of significant harm. Court proceedings in such situations were often fraught, lasting several days and could involve cross-examination by three or four different sets of barristers, all seeking to undermine my professional credibility and the evidence base informing my assessment.

I'm reminded of all this when teaching the importance of sound evidence-based assessments and 'defensible decision-making', alongside analytical thinking, writing and verbal expression.

Keeping the needs and welfare of that vulnerable child or young person central ensured an ability to stay strong, focused and determined in the witness box. A key factor in retaining the emotional resilience to withstand the onslaught was a supportive team - and a Friday night out in a Derbyshire pub.

As the taxi took us to our various homes we would pile coins into the hands of Jackie, the last on the run.

*David chose **Budget** (Southwark Financial Review 1974-75) ...*

... because this Social Services Budget reflects the transition to the new world in UK social work, following the *Seebohm Report*.

You may be surprised that social services for 250,000 people were provided for by only £9.6 million (£70-75m in today's money): Southwark, a London Borough, now spends two and a half times that.

So much for Seebohm's assertion 'that these changes have no financial implications'.

Looking at the composition of the budget, there is a mix of the old and the new. The first line of the budget announces that £1 million was spent on generic fieldwork – the new Seebohm 'big idea'.

Further down, sums are listed for the traditional welfare services. More is spent on each of homes for children and for the elderly than on fieldwork. Domiciliary services also take a chunk of the money.

Sheltered employment, and day and training centres still figure large. It is notable that fieldwork came in under-budget: there was a young, bright and committed workforce, but there weren't enough social workers to go round.

This was the first of the all-too-frequent reorganisations that beset UK social work over the coming years; and it was a time before the uncritical outsourcing and poorly exercised privatisations of later years.

David Whiting
In 1971, I was elected to Southwark Council for what I'd thought was an unwinnable ward. At the time I worked in the marketing department of IPC Business Press. I identified a gap in the market for a serious professional magazine and this work led to the launch of 'Community Care'. Since 1987 I've run my own publishing house, Whiting and Birch.

1974/75 Actual £	NET EXPENDITURE
1,014,630	Fieldwork
6,534	Pre School Playgroups
280,170	Day Nurseries
110,370	Day Care Centre for Children
332,188	Meals Service
229,300	Day Centres for the Elderly
67,185	Day Centres for the Mentally Ill
109,701	Training Centres for the Mentally Handicap
23,168	Sheltered Employment and Blind Homewo
801,273	Home Help
32,722	Services in the Home
73,932	Domiciliary Supportive Services
93,946	Preventive and Supportive Services
75,558	Miscellaneous Supportive Services
108,992	Boarding Out
4,702	Intermediate Treatment
14,390	Training of Houseparents
145,384	Reception Homes for Children
1,252,206	Children's Homes
86,195	Children's Hostels
197,374	Approved Schools
77,176	Community Homes with Closed Provision
1,270,767	Homes for the Elderly
76,232	Homes for the Physically Handicapped Blin
34,615	Homes for Mentally Handicapped Children
85,650	Homes for Mentally Handicapped Adults
57,000	Homes for the Mentally Ill
6,409	Mother and Baby Homes
184,286	General Transport
754,017	Social Services Administration
14,990	Research and Development
–	Reserve for Statutory Responsibilities
	Contingencies
£7,621,062	Committee Total Transferred to G.R.F. Summary

COMMUNICATING SOCIAL WORK

COMMUNICATING SOCIAL WORK *COLLECTION*

notebooks

My student note-books from all three years capture my learning journey, reminding me how privileged I was to have access to the lives of the people I worked with; each one of them moulded me into who I am now. I think everyone would benefit from a little notebook.

Amanda Taylor

radio

Like radio, social work must be in tune with its public, listening to what it has to say.
Also like radio, social work must offer choice and stay connected to the world to keep up to date, in order to achieve success with its educational and awareness mission.

Ginette Berteau

computer

Social workers and computers have a deeply ambivalent love/hate relation-ship. Instruments of managerialism? Or agent for profound social change and unparalleled profe-ssional networking? Social work's relationship with the shape-shifting computer is always on the move.

Neil Ballantyne

iPod

My iPod (with head phones) allows me to shut off from the open plan office whilst recording. Used in conjunction with my car stereo, it's an ice breaker with young people - 'find us a tune to listen to' can be disarming and an excuse for them to slag off your collection!

Patrick Donohue

baby monitor

Many people I've worked with as a social worker desc-ribe being anxious over someone they care for, causing sleeplessness.
Baby monitors allow people to stay in their own bed and get a better quality sleep, so affording a sense of relief and also of personal dignity.

Marion Robbins

selfie

Unity is a group of social work service users and carers in Stirling, Scotland. We teach social work and nursing students and contribute to university and other events like open days and conferences. Social work is about people and it is about involvement.

We took this Selfie at one of our meetings, and not everyone was there. This made us think about the limitations of a 'snapshot' to represent who we are and what we do. We think that it is important for Unity, and also for social work, to recognise the missing voices and try to draw these in.

The Unity Group

*Nicki chose **Mobile phone** ...*

... because it has become a conduit for my personal and professional development in ways that I couldn't have imagined at the start of my career.

Who can ignore the cultural and historical significance of the mobile phone, changing the way we communicate and socialise?

My trusty little phone helps me to celebrate my family and friend relationships when I can't be there in person, keeping the people that I love close. This has been so very important in this first year after qualification, which has been an intensive, emotional and demanding time.

My mobile phone enhances my professional identity. I access forums, read posts and engage in discussions with other social workers. I feel part of a community that I take with me throughout the day. I gain advice and guidance about practice, read commentary and critique of policies that impact upon my role, and learn about the development of legislation and case law.

I find excitement and inspiration about social work through the information available to me instantaneously and continuously, and feel solidarity with other professionals learning and sharing their experiences across the world.

I've come to realise the importance of self-care and my need to find creative outlets. With my mobile, I take pictures and share them with people, listen to music while I run, follow a guided meditation, do a yoga class when I need to wind down.

I'd literally be lost without it, thanks to the satnav app.

Nicki Musgrove
I'm a newly qualified social worker. I'd tried various stuff; freelance photography, hospitality, bar work; but working with young people in the voluntary sector ignited the spark to be a social worker. The training was the most challenging, intense, emotional journey of my life. Now I work in a 'permanance' team.

GIFTS AND MEMENTOES

GIFTS AND MEMENTOES *COLLECTION*

book stand	letter opener	cane	bard on a brick	ceramic	esculape

book stand

As a trainee social worker I wrote a Court report on a lad who'd been in trouble. At the conclusion of our work he shyly presented me with this book stand he'd made himself.

The family's poverty had shocked me, but their warmth and humanity moved me.

Julie Mann

letter opener

I was working with a woman who was severely psychotic. One Christmas she appeared at the door with a roughly wrapped present: 'a letter opener for all them letters you get'. It was a fire poker! I treasure it still. Even with so little, she wanted to say thank you in her own way.

Jim Monach

cane

This cane belonged to Arthur, a man with schizophrenia who died of cancer while I was working with him. He used his cane for balance problems. I keep it to remind me of the importance of advocating for people with no voice, and who are so often not seen as whole *people*.

Mary E. Garrison

bard on a brick

The bard was a corner stone of a workhouse that became a geriatric hospital offering no privacy. I was involved in its closure and replacement by more modern, open facilities. I kept the stone as a reminder of the part social workers have played in closing big institutions.

Ray Jones

ceramic

This ceramic sculpture is a mosaic of small blue and white circles made by people with learning disabilities in Cambridge.

It has pride of place in our living room. It symbolises for me the oft-neglected strengths of people with learning disabilities.

Shula Ramon

esculape

This bronze figure was given to me by a Dutch colleague. Esculape is the god of healing, which appeals to my interest in loss and grief. The figures provide support (are they holding up the world?) and they seem to merge into one, as if to say how much stronger we are together.

Neil Thompson

Postman Pat is a character from a children's animation that first appeared on BBC in 1981.

kembang

Kembang (Blossom) was painted by Siti Atiqah, a 16 yr old artist with cerebral palsy in supported employment in Malaysia. When I feel down about Western social work I remind myself of these and similar ventures providing disadvantaged people with real work.

Sara Ashencaean Crabtree

*Sheila chose **Postman Pat** ...*

... because this model was hand-crafted by one of my sons when he was 5 or 6 years old. 'Patrick' came to work with me and has been a permanent feature on my social work desk for around 30 years. I have had him with me as a constant reminder that although I have been duty bound to take the needs of other people's children as being paramount, within my personal life 'my own boys' always had priority.

Managing child care and protection issues as a professional worker and balancing this with my own parenting was always a complicated process which invariably involved issues of guilt and self-doubt. Guilt regarding the 'mum' space in my head being used to think about child care cases when I was at home being a mum, and self-doubt around the assessment of what was 'good enough' parenting for the children I was working with.

Patrick is symbolic of this emotional experience and is also a reminder that although social work can never be termed a 9 to 5 job, it is okay to have a life as well.

My first work was with the Deaf and Hearing impaired community in Aberdeen. I carried a 'generic' caseload, so met and worked with a wide variety of service users.

Currently I'm Course Leader for the Practice Learning Qualification, so I engage with social workers who are keen to become involved in practice education.

Sheila Slesser

Gerry Heery

Growing up in Belfast during the troubles, I knew nothing about social work until a charity group visited my school to recruit volunteers to work with 'disadvantaged people'. That summer experience led me to ditch my proposed economics degree for social work. Then I told my parents!

*Gerry chose **Crib** ...*

... because it was made for me by Peter, a young person I worked with early in my social work career.

Growing up as a member of the Nationalist community in Northern Ireland during a time of communal violence has surely influenced my practice in aspects I may never fully understand.

When Peter made the crib I was living in an area which had experienced several murders and attacks on peoples' homes, as it was a border area between the two main communities.

I had to leave my family home, which has since been demolished; in its place is a large 30 foot 'peace wall'.

Like all social workers in N. Ireland I had to find ways to work with all sections of our society. I was privileged to work with some colleagues in imaginative and creative ways, seeking to contribute to peace and reconciliation.

As well as the crib, I still have a photo of me with Peter and two other young men I was working with, as their Probation Officer in West Belfast, and known for several years. Within ten years they were all dead. One took his own life, another was shot in a paramilitary feud and the third, Peter, who made the crib, died of alcohol abuse.

Social work often entails working with the misery, the trauma and the tragedy in other people's lives. It is crucial that we recognize the impact of such events and find ways to look after ourselves, too.

Paul Guckian

In 1989 I was appointed as sole social worker to Our Lady's Psychiatric Hospital in Co. Clare, Ireland. It opened in 1868 as the county Lunatic Asylum and closed in 2002.

A certain status was attached to the ownership of the keys which opened (and locked) the female and male admissions wards.

Paul chose Keys (female & male) ...

... because many service users spoke of their negative experiences as the key-holder admitted them to the ward and their distress as the large doors were locked behind them.

Legislation and practice has moved on since Ireland's mental health laws were found to be in breach of the European Convention of Human Rights.

The emphasis now is a community-based Recovery model and a rights-based approach. I am no longer sole social worker but head up a full team of practitioners.

To this day I carry these keys on me at all times as a reminder of times past and a warning that even in our modern approach, we ought not to forget issues of power and control, and need to maintain a constant vigilance that key pads and swipe cards do not become the keys of the modern era.

NATURAL WORLD

I first encountered social services in 1954. I was five years old.

Bella

35

Some ladies came to our house and took me, my 3 year old sister and my one year old brother away from my mother, out of our house, down the cobbled street lined with curious neighbours and into two waiting cars.

I never saw my mother again.

This surely can't have been the first contact with social services, but for us it was a bolt out of the blue. We were terrified. We were never told why we were being taken into care, either then or later. I despised my mother until I was in my twenties, believing that she had simply abandoned us, as she never came to see us.

One day much later, during a visit to the matron of the children's home who was then long retired, she casually remarked that the 'powers that be' had decided that when we were taken into care my mother should not be allowed to see us. Matron said my mother turned up often in the first few months and would get hysterical before being sent away, but eventually gave up coming. How cruel.

Life in the children's home was mixed.

Christmas was good; we got presents and we didn't mind at all that they were second-hand. Bonfire Night was always brilliant: fireworks, special food (Matron made wonderful toffee) and jacket potatoes from the bonfire once it had died down and the 'Guy' which we had lovingly dressed and stuffed with straw had burned to a crisp.

I contacted my friend June with whom I grew up in the children's home. We both agreed our 'Object' had to be our Boxer dog, Bella. We all loved Bella and Bella loved all of us – always, indiscriminately and lavishly. She was a wonderful dog, placid and gentle and endlessly affectionate. The terror of postmen, she would always try (and sometimes succeeded) in biting them, which we knew was quite simply further proof of her love, devotion and desire to protect us.

She could do no wrong in our eyes.

So, beautiful **Bella**, you epitomised unconditional love and acceptance, a wonderful antidote to the emotional austerity of life in a children's home in Yorkshire in the 1950s and 60s.

Joan Cawston

*Pascal chose a super-hero character **The Falcon** ...*

... because he is the reason why I became a social worker. When I was a child, I used to read lots of comics and I was particularly interested by this character: he was the sidekick of Captain America and I always have been fascinated by Number 2's because of my personal story. In the 'real' life, The Falcon's alter ego, Sam Wilson, is in fact a social worker and I had no idea of what this meant. I remember enquiring and thinking 'Oh, helping people, this is the coolest job in the world!'.

I loved the complementarity of saving people literally as a superhero and saving them metaphorically as a social worker. The Falcon is able to fly, which is also something I do in my night dreams and in my day dreams, with a lot of consistency. He is able to connect to birds and see through their eyes which is also something I can do as a social worker – I see through the eyes of the street children of India.

For some reason, they have not chosen me to play the role in The Avengers movie but there is no doubt: I am The Falcon.

Pascal Fautrat

I am a social worker in New Delhi, India. I founded TARA Homes, which rescues, shelters and educates children in need of care and protection. I originate from France, where I studied social work, psychology and project management. Ten years ago, I was on holidays in India and I stepped by accident on a 4 years old child living on the pavement. I decided to stay in India and to start my own NGO to take care of street children. I never returned to my country of origin and feel I am one of the luckiest people in the world.

NATURAL WORLD *COLLECTION*

fish net	trees	bonsai	cork

fish net

Post-modern culture is a network culture. Fish net symbolises the connections between public and private sectors, teamwork, social partnerships and social clustering.

Fostering individual identity whilst accepting difference is a real challenge that networks can help to meet.

Giedrė Kvieskienė

trees

Trees are my metaphor for social work. They stand tall, reaching outward and up-ward, roots firmly planted in the ground. They are flexible, swaying in harsh storms. They provide shelter and habitat. They are various and have most prominence standing together.

Edna Cromer

bonsai

Bonsai represents the art of the possible. My experience in social work, especially when I was in political office in Croatia, showed me that social work is also the art and science of the possible. It must be engaged, political, ambitious, always the next best.

Nino Žganec

cork

Cork is a good metaphor for social work in many ways: it's sustainable in the way social workers help clients to be self-sustaining - it insulates, like the warmth and unconditional posit-ive regard of social work. It dampens sound, like social workers absorb what clients say.

Racheal Johnston

DYSTOPIA / UTOPIA

The Yellow star is a symbol of the holocaust.

Jo Finch
I grew up in a single parent family at a time when there was shame and stigma, but I knew that my family wasn't 'broken'. I had a radical education and it was inevitable I'd become a social worker as there was no other profession where I could 'live' my politics.

*Jo chose **Yellow star** ...*

... because it is a stark reminder of how 'caring' professions like social work can become caught up in ideological systems that breach fundamental human rights.

Some of social work's roots are deeply uncomfortable: a Victorian moralising discourse of the deserving and the undeserving, and the Eugenics movement, with concerns about 'lunatics' and 'the feeble-minded' breeding. Eugenics was influential in US social work practice, with a focus on 'mental and social hygiene'. The forced sterilisation of those with learning disabilities was a common practice.

In Nazi Germany, social workers, alongside others such as social pedagogues, submitted documents to courts that detailed 'concerns' about children seen as delinquent, disabled, mentally ill or not racially pure. Social workers worked in institutions where the killing of these 'degenerates' was commonplace.

It would be comforting to think inhumane practice was a thing of the past, but as recently as 1970, aboriginal children in Australia were forcibly removed from their homes and placed with white families.

This is the dark side of social work, one where the profession acts as an agent of the state, whatever its ideology.

Our ultimate goal has to be to challenge all social injustice and inequality, uphold human rights and be advocates for those whose voice is silenced by a conspiring system.

Most importantly, we need to worry whether practices of today will be the scandals of the future.

A Dalek is a creation from the BBC science fiction programme, 'Dr Who'. Frightening though Daleks were, they couldn't go up stairs! (Since then Daleks have learned to levitate.)

Jill chose **Dalek** ...

... because to me it exemplifies the Social Model of Disability – or for the layman:

If you get the environment right it minimizes the problems.

The biggest problem we face in our prisons is that most are not adapted for disabled people; the cell doors are too narrow for wheelchairs, there are no accessible showers, it can be difficult to get grab rails or a raised toilet seat, and there are stairs EVERYWHERE with no lifts. Hence the Dalek.

Dalek also epitomises the frustrations of the job; of still having to have these arguments; of legislation (the Care Act) being introduced with no thought about what adaptations are needed to prisons; of working with people who 'don't agree with disabled prisoners getting special treatment'.

Jill Palmer

I began my working life as a nurse. After a diversion by way of managing a music shop, I became home care coordinator in London, in the days before outsourcing, then a care manager in the physical disabilities team. Croydon borough funded me for a DipSW qualification. I've had a varied career: a hospital social worker; in a mental health team; an adults community team; HIV social worker and currently with disabled prisoners in Yorkshire.

Valérie Roy
I grew up in a Catholic family and one of my uncles was a missionary in S. America. He was very devoted to his community, especially poor families and political prisoners. At 8 years old, I didn't know anything about social work, but I sure wanted be a missionary too, in order to help people. Now I'm Professeure at École de service social at Université Laval in Québec.

*Valérie chose **Cross** ...*

... because, though it may be a delicate or controversial symbol, for me it shows similar complexities with social work.

This image of the cross looks like a pendant I had at the time I knew my uncle (I've looked for the original Cross and can't find it – some Objects go missing!)

As I grew up, my religious beliefs have progressively given way to a secular commitment, but I always kept this motivation to serve others.

Serving others refers to a debate in Québec about the designation of social work itself, whether it should be called *service social* (social service) or *travail social* (social work).

This debate goes back to the religious roots of social work in Québec's francophone context. At the time, the first forms of social work in Québec's anglophone community were secular, while for the franco-phone community, they were carried by different Catholic organizations. I personally consider that the idea to 'work with people', which is an important value in social work, is better translated by the designation *travail social;* however, I have a personal and historical attachment to the designation *service social* because of these roots.

Alternatively, the cross also symbolizes for me a darker side of social work, namely the power social workers can have over people and the potential abuses of 'acting in the name of' or 'for the good of others'.

Even if we work *with* people and even if we adopt a critical and reflexive practice, I don't think we can escape from these risks as we are all human beings.

Therefore, ethics and regulatory systems are essential in order to protect people from our power and to ensure that we serve them without any personal or professional prejudice.

*Jorūnė chose **Candle** ...*

... because it is a symbol that contains one of the meanings I think social work also has – to bring hope and light to a person's life.

As *candle,* a social worker shines light on situations that seem discouraging. It can be compared to a situation when you sit in a dark room and cannot see anything around until somebody brings in the lighted candle. When people have dark times and crises in their lives, often everything can seem lost, without any possible solutions. It is the social worker who can enlighten, help people to look around and discover the possibility that there are so many different ways to see yourself, your family and the world.

A candle has many meanings of hope and light for me. When you are stuck in a tunnel, the light from a candle helps you find a way out. A candle shines not just on the outside world but the inside world as well. You can be lost in your 'inner tunnel' and the candle's light gives you hope and strength to see lightness in your own soul. And to see that life's circumstances can be changed.

Social workers bring this 'candle' to others to enlighten their lives.

Jorūnė Vyšniauskytė-Rimkienė

I came to social work not knowing much about what it was but feeling that it was my field. In Lithuania before my studies began, social work did not exist. I was ten years in practice – in a school, and several NGOs with youth groups and communities. Now I teach at Vytautas Magnus university in Kaunas and at the same time work in the field as a groupworker.

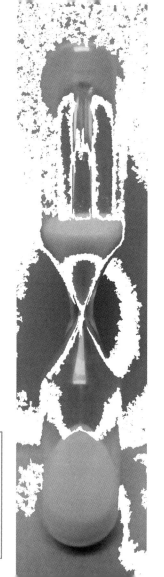

*Greg chose **Hour glass** ...*

... because it's an object that measures time passing, unstoppably, until time runs out.

Is time beginning to run out for social workers and other helping professionals? Time running out to deter the developing crisis of mass victimizations through shootings, bombings and other methods we are witnessing increasingly in the past decade in the global community. Throughout our history, social workers have contributed to the confrontation and defeat of hateful and destructive social and political forces, but in recent times we have seen violence increasing in frequency and scope, with no clear sign of a path to relief or resolution.

While social work is an absolutely necessary component of the arsenal with which we must confront violent global forces, my concern grows that social workers and other helping professionals cannot slow the passage of time as it runs unstoppably toward the triumph of these violent global forces. Do social workers have the necessary knowledge, skills and resources to confront and conquer these violent forces that, like the hour glass, seem unstoppable?

I hope so.

Greg Tully
After many years as an athlete I began sports coaching. I decided I wanted to affect people's lives more deeply in a profession that addressed values of justice and fairness. As a social worker I practised advocacy and counselling, especially with victims of violence and with communities addressing violence. I'm now a university professor and President of the International Association for Social Work with Groups.

DYSTOPIA / UTOPIA

band aid	insurances	walking stick	pen	umbrella	heart
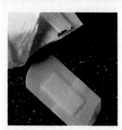		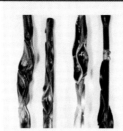			

band aid

I feel that much of social work goes to mending and fixing individuals. This is often inadequate when the need is for social reform. It's trying to move a mountain with a spoon. I'd like more emphasis on community organizing, policy change and action to promote social justice.

Barbara Friesen

insurances

I love counselling work, but it's the insurance companies that decide who I can work with.
I have to employ someone to process cumbersome paperwork which goes unpaid for ages.
It's wrong that these companies determine who I can see and what social work is.

Marsha Pilz

walking stick

Social work is like a walking stick that aids people with life's journey when they have been injured by other people, circumstances or the past. It takes the pressure off their injury so it can heal.
These walking sticks look sturdy, yet imperfect - just like social workers.

Nicole Liebenberg

pen

Like a pen, social workers leave a mark on the people whose lives they touch.
Our 'ink' doesn't last forever and we need refilling from time to time, which I've found one of the biggest challenges social workers face. Self-care helps with my ink levels.

Evadné van den Berg

umbrella

Social work can provide the shelter of an 'umbrella' for people when they most need it - and perhaps prevent them seeking inappropriate cover - the social work umbrella helps people to weather their own personal storms and to know that they are not alone.

Dete Kelder

heart

The heart is a symbol for the truest kind of wisdom - emotional intelligence. This generates empathy and openness with clients, seeing the world from their perspective, so they feel safe, valued and accepted. I check my personal 'Heart' before every encounter.

Jurgita Kupriūnienė